Baseball Sensation

SportStars
Volume 2

Baseball Sensation

SportStars
Volume 2

A Biography By
Christine Dzidrums
Photos By Joseph Dzidrums

CREATIVE MEDIA, INC.
PO Box 6270
Whittier, California 90609-6270
United States of America

www.CreativeMedia.net

Cover and Book design by Joseph Dzidrums
Cover photos by Joseph Dzidrums

First Edition: July 2013

Library of Congress Control Number: 2013912514

ISBN 978-1-938438-28-8   10 9 8 7 6 5 4 3 2 1

For Thomas Wayne Allison,
A Future Angels Fan

Special Thanks
Jeff Allison
Joseph Dzidrums
Jennifer Varley
JRoadie1
Joshua, Timmy and Ashley

Table of Contents

"I'm really close to my parents."

BABY TROUT

On August 7, 1991, expectant mother Debbie Trout awoke with labor pain. She sat up in bed and squinted at the blurry numbers on her alarm clock. Her contractions felt very strong. Could labor have accelerated so quickly?

"Jeff," she whispered, nudging her husband. "Wake up. The baby is on his way."

Moments later, the young couple scrambled about their modest home, preparing for a hospital visit. As Debbie threw on comfortable clothes and grabbed her maternity suitcase stacked with newborn diapers and baby clothes, Jeff arranged babysitting preparations for their two children. Five-year-old Teal and three-year-old Tyler snoozed soundly in their beds. The siblings would soon welcome their baby brother into their lives.

A few minutes later, Debbie sat in the passenger seat of the family car as her husband zipped briskly through the streets of Vineland, New Jersey. The anxious mother-to-be sucked in a sharp breath as another contraction signaled that her son was quickly on his way. She glanced anxiously at the vehicle's clock. It was nearly 4 a.m. Her contractions were coming faster and lasting longer. Would they make it to Newcomb Hospital in time? Teal and Tyler's labors had been lengthy processes, but her newest child seemed impatient to enter the world.

"Slow down, little one," she willed silently, gripping the car's armrest as another contraction arrived.

When the parents-to-be arrived at the hospital, personnel whisked them into Labor and Delivery. A nurse examined Debbie and discovered that her baby was ready to be born! A doctor was summoned to deliver her son.

Just three hours later, a blissful Debbie and Jeff took turns cradling their baby boy. They named their son: Michael Nelson Trout. Little did the emotional parents know that in eighteen years' time, over 45,000 people would chant their son's name on a daily basis.

Eyeing a Pop-up
(Joseph Dzidrums)

Michael Nelson Trout
(Joseph Dzidrums)

"You have to stay humble. That's what my parents always taught me as a kid – not to get cocky, not to get a big head."

Chapter One

TEE BALL TO HIGH SCHOOL

Jeff Trout loved playing sports, particularly baseball. As a teenager the Minnesota Twins selected him in the fifth round of the 1983 draft. He worked his way through the team's minor league system and advanced as high as Class AA ball for the Orlando Twins, two steps away from Major League Baseball. A solid hitter, the second baseman remained in the minors for four seasons, but it wasn't a life of luxury. If the big leagues represent money, glamour and fame with private jets, exotic food and posh hotel rooms, the minors embody the opposite of their big brother.

"You leave the ballpark at midnight, ride seven hours on a bus, get into the next town in the morning, sleep a little then get ready to play at night," Jeff later recalled to *ESPN*. "I remember so many nights of not sleeping and looking out the windows of the bus seeing rows of cornfields."

When Jeff eventually retired due to a nagging knee injury, he married a pretty blonde named Debbie. The happy couple settled in Vineland, New Jersey. In five short years, they welcomed three children into their lives. Their lone daughter, Teal, arrived in 1986. The pretty brunette adored playing softball. Tyler entered the world in 1988. The stellar athlete excelled at golf. In 1991 Mike's birth completed the family. Like his siblings, he loved playing sports, especially baseball.

The content family eventually moved to nearby Millville, New Jersey, a small, blue-collar town, and purchased a two-story home on a quiet cul-de-sac. Jeff began teaching history at the local high school and coached the football and baseball teams, too. The devoted father often brought Mike to baseball practices, watching in amusement as his precocious two-year-old zipped around the bases. Boy, the kid could run!

"He was always around the field, players and practices," Jeff told the *Orange County Register*. "He'd want to be in the action."

When Mike turned five years old, his parents enrolled him in a tee ball league. The excited youngster loved smashing the ball with his bat, running quickly and firing a baseball.

A few years later Mike joined a Little League baseball team. Unlike the simplistic tee ball, he now faced a pitcher rather than hitting the ball off of a tee. Because the youngster admired New York Yankees shortstop Derek Jeter, he wore number two, just like his idol. The active child loved everything about baseball: hitting, running, catching, throwing and stealing bases. Mike also enjoyed forging friendships with teammates. On nights before a game, the eager ballplayer felt so excited that he wore his uniform to bed!

Although Mike had many friends while growing up, he felt very close to his two siblings. During cold weather days, the threesome often played board games, like Scrabble or Monopoly. The younger brother took every game seriously, expressing great disappointment when he didn't win. When the weather permitted, the children played outdoors and turned the family backyard into their personal baseball diamond, even creating makeshift bases.

"We can use Mom's flip flop for home plate," Teal suggested.

"I brought Dad's jacket for second base," Tyler announced.

Although the older Trout children were very athletic, they often felt resigned when facing their extremely talented younger brother. Teal and Tyler groaned in frustration when Mike walked up to the plate and waved his bat confidently while waiting for someone to pitch the wiffle ball. He usually smashed the plastic ball into the corner of the backyard and rounded the bases in a well-rehearsed home run trot.

"Mikey used to beat us all the time," Teal revealed to *TheDailyJournal.com.* "We wouldn't even try to get him out. He was always the best hitter, and always the fastest."

Before long Mike joined a traveling baseball team and trekked across New Jersey and Pennsylvania to compete against other talented players. The adolescent imagined himself as a Major League Baseball player playing in a large stadium, while thousands of screaming fans chanted his name.

Millville, New Jersey

Mike Meets His Idol: Derek Jeter
(Jennifer Varley)

On weekends, Mike and his father watched sports on television. The mesmerized child could watch entire baseball games without growing restless. He always cheered for the Philadelphia Phillies, and their All-Star shortstop Jimmy Rollins and second baseman Chase Utley. During basketball season, he rooted for the NBA's Philadelphia 76ers and their star Allen Iverson.

On Mike's 12th birthday his dad took him to Yankee Stadium for a day game. Father, son and 51,000 plus fans watched Derek Jeter, Bernie Williams and Mike Mussina defeat the Texas Rangers in a come-from-behind 7-5 victory. The awe-struck adolescent studied the professional players carefully. He felt certain that the hard-working athletes had the best job in the world!

Shortly after Mike's 15th birthday, he started his freshman year at Millville High School. The 5'9", 160 pounder played baseball, football and basketball. Whatever the sport, every time the dedicated athlete put on his orange and blue uniform, he vowed to give 100%.

The savvy sportsman even used basketball to improve his performance on the baseball diamond. The grueling game kept him in top shape and increased his already impressive speed. Wearing number 10, the power forward led the state in steals during his junior and senior years.

"He played every second like it was the last second he would play," raved his coach, Dale Moore.

"I don't think it would matter what he played," he continued. "If it was tennis, golf, darts, he would give it his all. As soon as he put that uniform on, all he would think about is doing what he could do to help us win."

Although Mike maintained a solid grade point average while juggling after-school sports, he led a fulfilling social life, as well. The high school student began dating a classmate named Jessica Cox and considered the blonde, blue-eyed beauty his very best friend.

"We trust each other," Mike later told the *Philadelphia Daily News*. "She is somebody I can talk to and is always here for me."

With two parents working in the teaching profession, Mike understood the importance of a solid education. An injury could end his participation in sports forever, but knowledge lasted a lifetime. The youngest Trout treated his teachers respectfully, completed his homework and studied hard.

"One of my proudest moments was when Mike made the National Honor Society," Jeff told the *Orange County Register*. "His success in school and knowing that he was a respectful, humble kid were most important to us."

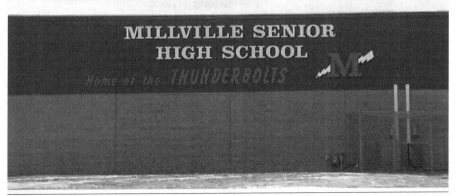

Mike filled his parents' hearts with pride on the baseball field, too. The hardworking competitor made the varsity team during his freshman year. Wearing number one on his jersey, he was a strong pitcher, clocking a fastball as high as 91 miles per hour. During his junior year he threw a no-hitter and posted an 8-2 record with a 1.77 ERA and 124 strikeouts. As a hitter, Mike fared even better, batting .530 with 9 home runs and 35 RBIs.

These remarkable stats prompted Coach Roy Hallenbeck to move Mike to the outfield during his senior year. If he produced terrific offensive numbers while juggling pitching duties, how much stronger could his hitting become if he focused on it exclusively?

Hallenbeck's decision paid off handsomely. The Thunderbolts' newest center fielder set a state record for most home runs (19) in one season. Mike also produced a career-best offensive season, netting a .531 batting average, 49 runs, 45 RBIs, 6 doubles, 1 triple and 19 stolen bases.

One day as Jeff watched Mike play ball, he noticed a young man videotaping his son. His curiosity piqued, the father approached the fan.

"What are you doing?" he asked.

"I'm videotaping him," the man replied. "I want to sell the footage on *eBay* one day when he's famous."

The videographer wasn't the only person interested in Mike. Universities sent letters of interest on a daily basis. If the young ball player wanted, he could attend college on a full scholarship. After mulling through many offers, Mike verbally committed to East Carolina University in Greenville, North Carolina.

Not so fast, though! Major League Baseball scouts had begun noticing Mike, too. In particular, representatives from the Los Angeles Angels of Anaheim and New York Yankees frequently attended Thunderbolt games to monitor the high school star. Both teams seemed extremely interested in signing Mike to a big league contract, and he wanted nothing more than to play professional baseball.

The Big "A"
(Joseph Dzidrums)

*"As soon as I sign,
I'm ready to go."*

Chapter Two

THE DRAFT

Mike Trout couldn't sleep. He felt exceedingly restless. It was June 9, 2009. On the very next day, the hot prospect would attend the Major League Baseball Annual Draft. He had spent the earlier part of the evening burning off anxiety on his PlayStation. Several hours into a marathon gaming session, the teenager opted to give sleep a shot. He lay in bed for over an hour before finally dozing.

When Mike awoke at 7:30 a.m., he felt edgy with antici-pation. In a few hours the Trouts would drive 126 miles north to the *MLB Network* studios in Secaucus, New Jersey, for base-ball's first televised draft, and he'd learn which Major League team would draft him. The responsible seventeen-year-old drove to school that morning, treating the date like any other school day. He attended morning classes and then chatted with Coach Hallenbeck for several minutes. Had the ball player wanted to ignore the draft, it wouldn't have been possible. Everywhere he went, classmates and teachers wished him luck.

Several hours later, a tense Mike arrived in Secaucus. Organizers escorted the Major League hopeful to a mock dug-out which served as the studio's set. Accompanied by his family and Jessica, the teen sat on a wooden bench and braced for an agonizingly long wait. It was then Mike learned that he was the only prospect to attend the proceedings. He tried to remain composed when the draft went live and television cameras cap-tured his every reaction.

It came as little surprise when the Washington Nationals, the first team to select a player, drafted college pitcher Stephen

Strasburg. The Seattle Mariners chose North Carolina's Dustin Ackley as the second pick, and a high school prodigy named Donavan Tate was selected third by the San Diego Padres.

Nearly an hour later, as Mike's father paced nervously in the faux dugout, the Angels readied to announce their pick. The Anaheim-based team had expressed interest in Mike for months, but would the 2002 World Series Champions show faith in him when it truly mattered? Television cameras zoomed in on Commissioner of Major League Baseball Bud Selig as he walked to the podium. The Trouts held their collective breath, awaiting potentially life-altering news.

"With the 25th selection in the 1st round of the 2009 First-Year Player Draft, the Los Angeles Angels of Anaheim select Michael Trout."

The studio audience burst into robust applause and cheers. A beaming Mike hugged his emotional mother and father. Anaheim's newest Angel worked his way down a line of supporters until he had embraced every family or friend in attendance. Moments later Millville's golden boy proudly wore an Angels cap while he addressed reporters.

"I'm so excited," Mike smiled. "[The Angels] have a good winning history. They're a good program and I can't wait to go out and play ball."

"We couldn't be more pleased," Jeff told *CBSSports.com*. "The Angels are a solid, winning organization and the reason why they pick late every year is because they're in the playoffs."

On June 16th, Mike celebrated another milestone when he marched in Millville High School's graduation ceremony. After four unforgettable years, the teenager graduated with a solid grade point average. He'd also carved an impressive basketball resume and established himself as one of the school's all-time great baseball talents.

Of Millville High School's entire graduating body, Mike was likely the only millionaire. For signing with the Angels, the slugger earned a 1.2 million dollar signing bonus. Yet for the time being, he didn't concern himself with his financial boon. Instead the ecstatic teen spent his grad night celebrating with loved ones.

And one day the baseball world would celebrate Mike Trout – and a lot sooner than anyone ever anticipated.

Angels: 2002 World Series Champions
(Joseph Dzidrums)

"If you get a negative thought in your head, you're probably going to fail."

Chapter Three

MINOR LEAGUE BASEBALL

The Trouts were a close-knit family. No matter how many miles Mike traveled, or how high his star might ascend, he would always need his family. For now, though, the minor was truly bound to his parents, legally. The underage baseball draftee's parents were required to cosign his professional contract!

Now that Mike was a big leaguer, he required monetary advisors. Craig Landis, a former minor league pitcher, signed on as the athlete's agent. His impressive client list included: Paul Konerko, Aaron Rowand and Brett Myers. The Trouts also hired a financial firm to invest Mike's money.

As Mike anticipated the momentous day when he would pack his bags and embark on a baseball career, he relaxed by enjoying many fishing outings. During the peaceful activity, the pensive teen mulled his future. What would life as a minor league baseball player be like?

Mike expected to remain in the minor league system for several years. Few players advanced to the big leagues quickly. Typically even the top prospects spent time at all three key levels, Class A, Class AA and Class AAA, before reaching the big leagues.

Because Jeff and Debbie had raised their children to be hard, humble workers, Mike's dad offered a frank description of minor league life. It was strenuous, low-paying and lonely. Yet the minors were also a gateway to euphoria - Major League Baseball.

Veterans Memorial Stadium - Cedar Rapids
(Betsy Wright)

In the spring of 2010 Mike received his first minor league assignment. He would play for the rookie level Arizona Angels. The brilliant phenom did not remain in Tempe, Arizona, long, though. Following a stellar debut that included a .360 batting average, management quickly elevated Mike to Class A ball.

For the 2010 baseball season, Mike primarily played for the Cedar Rapids Kernels. While playing in Iowa's second-largest city, the young player hit .362, smashed 6 home runs, recorded 39 runs batted in and stole 45 bases.

Thanks to Mike's outstanding efforts, *Baseball America* nominated him for the prestigious All-Star Futures Game. The popular exhibition game showcased minor league baseball's best players. It also occurrs during the same week as the Major League Baseball All-Star Game, an annual contest between the top American League and National League ball players.

As luck would have it, the Los Angeles Angels of Anaheim hosted that year's All-Star Game. Mike would have the unique opportunity to play in his future home, Angel Stadium of Anaheim! The eighteen-year-old entered the game as a pinch runner and assumed responsibilities in center field.

He went 2-4 at the plate, hitting a double and a single. His significant contributions helped lead the U.S. Futures to a 9-1 victory over the World Futures.

Mike remained in sunny Southern California following the All-Star Game, after the Angels promoted him to their Class A team, the Rancho Cucamonga Quakes, in the more competitive California League. While playing in San Bernardino County, Mike continued his winning ways and garnered several ardent fans. The popular player even enjoyed his own bobblehead night. By the season's end the teenager became the youngest player to ever win Topps Minor League Player of the Year honors.

In the spring of 2011, Mike arrived at the Angels spring training site in Tempe, Arizona, where he would train alongside many big leaguers. His veteran teammates couldn't resist having fun with him. They put the rookie through a time-honored hazing, where first-year players are forced to perform outlandish acts or wear ridiculous costumes in public. The Millville native was ordered to dress up as Lady Gaga, and looked quite the sight in a platinum blonde wig, black leather dress, sparkly shades and dangerously high heels!

"That was pretty intense," Mike later laughed.

During a game against the Oakland Athletics, pitcher Jered Weaver came up with the ultimate practical joke. The sly prankster gave Mike's cell phone number to the right-field scoreboard worker. Throughout the game, fans were invited to call the youngster directly with any questions. Needless to say, Mike changed his phone number after the game!

The upstart took the next logical step in his career when he began the baseball year with the Class AA team the Arkansas Travelers. Playing in historic Little Rock, Arkansas, Mike accumulated 412 plate appearances, 115 hits, 18 doubles, 13 triples, 11 home runs. 38 RBIs and 33 stolen bases.

The youngster's favorite part about the South? Storms. One afternoon Mike learned about a tornado brewing 20 miles from where he lived. The weather fan stayed outside watching the twister while his roommates took refuge inside.

"He's a weather geek," Jeff told the *Orange County Register*. "He'd probably be a storm chaser if he weren't playing baseball."

On July 8 at 2 a.m., Mike slept soundly in his apartment when the vibration from his cell phone interrupted a good dream. He reached for his phone and glanced at the caller ID. The phone number didn't look familiar, so he sent it to voice mail and fell back asleep. A minute later, his phone rang again. This time he answered. Angels General Manager Tony Reagins was on the other line. The team needed a center fielder and fast after Peter Bourjos sustained an injury. Mike was being promoted to the big leagues.

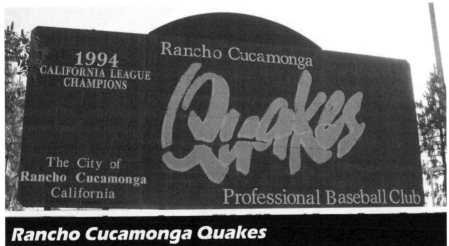

Rancho Cucamonga Quakes
(Joseph Dzidrums)

The Millville native sat up in bed. He nearly pinched himself. Was this a dream? Was he still asleep?

"Pack your bags," Reagins repeated. "You're flying to Anaheim."

Rancho Cucamonga Quakes
(Joseph Dzidrums)

"I always want to hit, but getting on base with a walk can be just as good."

Chapter Four

Major League Baseball

Less than 24 hours after being called up to the big leagues, an overwhelmed Mike Trout stepped onto the lush grass at Angel Stadium and surveyed his surroundings. A roaring crowd of 40,161 cheered on their newest player as he jogged to center field for his big-league debut. The precise second the home-plate umpire called, "Play ball!" and Seattle Mariner Ichiro Suzuki stepped into the batter's box, the Angels' newest rookie became the youngest player in Major League Baseball.

"I never felt like that before," Mike revealed to *MLB.com*. "Forty-thousand people just cheering you on. It was awesome."

Several hours earlier, Mike looked dazed when he entered the Angels clubhouse. Players he admired, like Tony Abreu, Torii Hunter and Mark Trumbo, stopped by his locker to welcome him to the big leagues. Moments later the rookie became emotional upon receiving his white and red #27 jersey.

Hitting in the ninth position, Mike struggled with the bat that night. He went 0 for 3 with two flyouts and a groundout. Despite his offensive woes, Mike still contributed in a big way during the top of the ninth inning. With the score tied at 3-3, Seattle's Franklin Gutierrez smashed a ball to right-center field. Showcasing his lightning speed, the rookie executed a phenomenal catch to rob the Mariner of a double. His terrific play kept the score tied until Mark Trumbo propelled the Angels to victory with a ninth-inning walk-off home run.

In the meantime, Jeff and Debbie Trout scrambled to book a flight to California, and a ride to the stadium, to catch their son's Major League debut. By the time the frazzled couple finally arrived at Angel Stadium, the game had already reached the eighth inning. As soon as the proud parents sat down, Mike made the memorable catch.

"Seeing him come off the field for the first time as a big leaguer getting a standing ovation was a pretty special moment," Jeff told the *Orange County Register*.

"Mike Trout's a legitimate center fielder," Angels manager Mike Scioscia raved. "There aren't many center fielders that have that much closing speed."

The following day a calmer Mike returned to the park and got his first Major League hit, an RBI bunt. When he reached first base, the coaching staff asked for the ball, so the new Angel could keep it as a memento. The nineteen-year-old would need to clear a lot more space on his trophy shelf. He was about to take Major League Baseball by storm.

Young Trout Fans
(Joseph Dzidrums)

Major League Baseball Player
(Joseph Dzidrums)

"I just go out there and do everything I can to win for the team."

Chapter Five

ALL-STAR

After the 2011 off-season, Mike took a much-needed break. He and his buddies sometimes cranked up a Brad Paisley tune and drove to Maurice River for a relaxing afternoon of fishing and crabbing. Sometimes the friends headed to their favorite Millville diner, where Mike has been known to wolf down six hamburgers in one sitting.

Mike used his free stretch to catch up with his family, too. On some occasions, the Trouts went golfing at their favorite course. Tyler had completed a business and economics degree and begun studying law at Rutgers, and Teal was married with two children. The baseball star adored spending quality time with his niece and nephew.

Of course Mike used his free nights to take Jessica on many dates. They ate at a steakhouse and then caught a flick at the town movie theater, where the Angel grabbed a tub of popcorn and snacked on his favorite candy, AirHeads. Sometimes the couple went bowling at their favorite spot, where the athlete once earned the coveted 300 score!

When the 2012 season arrived, Mike arrived at spring training intent on earning a spot on the Angels regular roster. His body, however, had other plans. Shortly after Mike's arrival, he came down with the dreaded stomach flu. Weakened by a staggering 23-pound weight loss, he struggled through February and March. If the illness wasn't difficult enough, he also suffered from tendonitis in his right shoulder.

As a result of his preseason obstacles, Mike Scioscia informed Mike that he would start the year with the Angels' Class AAA team, the Salt Lake Bees. Although the player felt disappointed with the assignment, he vowed to fight his way back to the big leagues.

"I'm going to be working hard every day and get back up here," he told his skipper.

Mike and seven other ball players rented a duplex in Salt Lake City, Utah. The four oldest athletes took one unit, while the rest lived in the other one. Mike bonded with his teammates and looked forward to their weekly barbecue. He loved roasting steak and eating spoonfuls of pal Luis Jimenez's Dominican rice.

Of course, Mike continued dazzling on the baseball field. Manager Keith Johnson described his star player as a good listener and a hard worker. The Bees' schedule included trips to such cities as Colorado Springs, Reno, Tucson, Sacramento and Tacoma. In the season's first 20 games, the slugger recorded a .403 batting average.

Mike's athletic exploits weren't lost on the Angels. In late April, the team summoned the hot hitter back to Anaheim, and the resolute teenager vowed his third trip to the majors would be his last. On June 4, he logged his first four-hit game, earning him shared American League Player of the Week honors with teammate Torii Hunter. Simultaneously, his defensive plays consistently awed spectators and aired on various sport networks' highlight reels. If all these accomplishments weren't impressive enough, baseball fanatics marveled at Mike's amazing speed on the base paths. Was there anything he couldn't do?

Manning the Outfield
(Joseph Dzidrums)

On July 1, Mike was named to his first All-Star team. He became the first Angel in history to make the Midsummer Classic without having been on the ballot! After all, when the voting sheets were initially printed, Mike was still playing in the minor leagues. Now he would actually be teammates with his childhood hero, Derek Jeter.

"It's awesome getting picked; getting chills thinking about it right now," Mike told the *Courier-Post*. "I'm just having fun. This is great."

"Making the All-Star team, it's a dream come true after all the hard work," he added.

Just a few days later, Mike flew to Kansas City, Missouri, for his first All-Star appearance. He grinned widely as he rode in a convertible alongside another phenom, Bryce Harper, during the All-Star Game Red Carpet Show. As baseball fans screamed and hollered his name, he shook his head in disbelief. The entire experience felt so surreal.

When Mike arrived for his first practice at Kaufmann Stadium, he could barely believe his eyes. His teammates featured a Who's Who of baseball legends. In addition to Jeter, the roster boasted Prince Fielder, David Ortiz, Justin Verlander and Miguel Cabrera. The smitten ballplayer began collecting his heroes' autographs. In the end, he walked away with many signed bats, jerseys and balls.

The weirdest part? Some veterans also asked Mike for his autograph! Despite the ultimate flattery, the player remained grounded.

Angel Stadium Entrance
(Joseph Dzidrums)

"Sometimes if you think about that stuff too much, you can get a big head, get a little cocky and I'm not like that," he remarked. "I try to stay humble."

In the end, the American League lost to the National League in an 8-0 rout. Nevertheless, Mike, who played left field, recorded a hit and a walk. For good measure, he also swiped a stolen base. It was a day the youth would never forget.

Back in his hotel room that night, Mike shuffled through his signed memorabilia. He would display most of the items in his special room back home. The 20-year-old had transformed his parents' basement into a man cave, featuring a sectional sofa, wet bar, 65-inch flat screen TV and assorted baseball paraphernalia.

"(Jeff) Weaver, and everybody else, gives me a hard time about still living at home," he grinned. "But I'm going to take advantage of it for as much as I can."

Now that Mike was an All-Star, his recognition factor soared. Fans often requested his autograph while he was at a restaurant or at the beach. Although the unassuming athlete missed his anonymity, he treated his fans kindly and generously.

During the baseball season, Mike and Garret Richards shared a condominium conveniently located down the street from Angel Stadium. The friends sometimes passed time by playing games on their PlayStation. Naturally they often challenged one another to *MLB: The Show*.

Although Mike had few competitors on the base paths, he eventually found something faster than him. The popular player bought a Mercedes AMG! A deluxe car featuring gull-wing doors, it boasted incredible speed.

With Bryce Harper in the All-Star Parade
(jroadie1)

After the All-Star break, Mike resumed his dream season. By the end of July, he became the first player to simultaneously snag Rookie of the Month and Player of the Month honors. The phenom also became Major League Baseball's youngest 30-30 member, an exclusive club for versatile players who have stolen 30 bases and smashed 30 home runs in one season. In addition, he also shattered Vladimir Guerrero's franchise record for most runs scored in a single year.

When 2012 officially ended, Mike could finally sit back and reflect on his astonishing season. The outfielder led the Angels in various categories: batting average, runs scored, hits, triples, stolen bases, walks, batting average, on-base percentage and slugging percentage.

On November 12, 2012, Mike became the youngest player ever to win the American League Rookie of the Year Award. Voted on by the Baseball Writers Association of America, the Angel joined illustrious past honorees, like Rod Carew, Derek Jeter, Mark McGwire and Cal Ripken Jr.

On the Scoreboard
(Joseph Dzidrums)

"To be a part of history at such a young age is especially rewarding and I am extremely humbled by it," he remarked.

Although many baseball players and sports fans believed that Mike should have won American League MVP honors, he fell just short of the award. Miguel Cabrera won the distinction instead, leading many to speculate that he received the nod because his team had made the playoffs, while the Angels did not. Regardless, Mike finished second in the voting and harbored no bitterness.

"To get to the big leagues last year and have a year like that, and to come second to the MVP, it's pretty incredible," he remarked. "It's a pretty crazy feeling."

In the end, the awards, while nice, were not as meaningful to Mike as the fact that his ultimate dream had come true. He was a professional baseball player. Mike Trout had arrived in the big leagues and he wasn't leaving anytime soon!

Manager Mike Scioscia (L)
(Joseph Dzidrums)

"It's a dream come true to be a Major League Baseball player."

Chapter Six

SUPERSTAR

Mike spent most of the off-season in Millville. He especially cherished spending the holidays with loved ones. His family had a tradition of placing Christmas trees in every room of the house. Pine-scented candles and bright, gift-wrapped boxes filled the cozy home. And the man who graced the cover of *Sports Illustrated*? He still received presents from Santa Claus!

When baseball season beckoned again, Mike began 2013 with a big bang. On April 20, the upstart stepped up to the plate during a rousing five-run first inning and smashed a ball over the center field wall for his first career grand slam. Fireworks exploded above Angel Stadium as the beloved star rounded the bases. His home run propelled the team to a 9-0 lead. Afterward the humble player remarked that he had hit, "just another home run."

About a month later, on what seemed like an ordinary night, Mike Trout nabbed an infield single after beating out the throw to first. He followed the hit with a triple in the very next inning. In his next at bat, he smashed a double into left field. Only a home run remained between him and the record books. If he hit a ball out of the park, he would become the youngest player in American League history to hit for the cycle, when a player achieves a single, double, triple and home run in one game.

In the eighth inning, Mike stepped in the batter's box with a shot at making history. Seattle Mariners pitcher Lucas

Luetge threw two straight balls out of the strike zone. Mike expected that the hurler would throw a strike next, or else he would find himself in a 3-0 hole. If he ever had a great shot at hitting a home run, it would come with the next pitch. Sure enough, Luetge threw a low fastball and Mike swung with all his might. The ball sailed high in the air toward the right-center field wall. Going, going, gone! Mike Trout had become the youngest American Leaguer to hit for the cycle! As the usually reserved player rounded the bases, he grinned and looked back at the outfield wall, almost in disbelief.

"It was in the back of my mind, trying to hit a home run," Mike told *USA Today*. "I just barreled it up and it went out. It feels great."

When Mike returned to the dugout, his teammates mobbed him. The crowd in attendance wasn't content to let the momentous milestone end just yet. Grandparents, moms, dads and children all whistled, applauded and stomped their feet until the treasured Angel ran back onto the field to take a curtain call. Upon seeing their hero, thousands of fans cheered with delight.

Yet for the humble Mike Trout, it was just another day on the baseball diamond. He was a baseball sensation!

Playing Center Field
(Joseph Dzidrums)

American League Rookies of the Year

2012: Mike Trout, Los Angeles Angels

2011: Jeremy Hellickson, Tampa Bay Rays
2010: Neftali Feliz, Texas Rangers
2009: Andrew Bailey, Oakland A's
2008: Evan Longoria, Tampa Bay Rays
2007: Dustin Pedroia, Boston Red Sox
2006: Justin Verlander, Detroit Tigers
2005: Huston Street, Oakland A's
2004: Bobby Crosby, Oakland A's
2003: Angel Berroa, Kansas City Royals
2002: Eric Hinske, Toronto Blue Jays
2001: Ichiro Suzuki, Seattle Mariners
2000: Kazuhiro Sasaki, Seattle Mariners
1999: Carlos Beltran, Kansas City Royals
1998: Ben Grieve, Oakland A's
1997: Nomar Garciaparra, Boston Red Sox
1996: Derek Jeter, New York Yankees
1995: Marty Cordova, Minnesota Twins
1994: Bob Hamelin, Kansas City Royals
1993: Tim Salmon, California Angels
1992: Pat Listach, Milwaukee Brewers
1991: Chuck Knoblauch, Minnesota Twins
1990: Sandy Alomar, Jr., Cleveland Indians
1989: Gregg Olson, Baltimore Orioles
1988: Walt Weiss, Oakland A's
1987: Mark McGwire, Oakland A's
1986: Jose Canseco, Oakland A's
1985: Ozzie Guillen, Chicago White Sox
1984: Alvin Davis, Seattle Mariners
1983: Ron Kittle, Chicago White Sox
1982: Cal Ripken, Baltimore Orioles
1981: Dave Righetti, New York Yankees
1980: Joe Charboneau, Cleveland Indians
1979: John Castino, Minnesota Twins and Alfredo Griffin,
Toronto Blue Jays
1978: Lou Whitaker, Detroit Tigers
1977: Eddie Murray, Baltimore Orioles
1976: Mark Fidrych, Detroit Tigers
1975: Fred Lynn, Boston Red Sox

At the Plate
(Joseph Dzidrums)

1974: Mike Hargrove, Texas Rangers
1973: Al Bumbry, Baltimore Orioles
1972: Carlton Fisk, Boston Red Sox
1971: Chris Chambliss, Cleveland Indians
1970: Thurman Munson, New York Yankees
1969: Lou Piniella, Kansas City Royals
1968: Stan Bahnsen, New York Yankees
1967: Rod Carew, Minnesota Twins
1966: Tommie Agee, Chicago White Sox
1965: Curt Blefary, Baltimore Orioles
1964: Tony Oliva, Minnesota Twins
1963: Gary Peters, Chicago White Sox
1962: Tom Tresh, New York Yankees
1961: Don Schwall, Boston Red Sox
1960: Ron Hansen, Baltimore Orioles
1959: Bob Allison, Washington Senators
1958: Albie Pearson, Washington Senators
1957: Tony Kubek, New York Yankees
1956: Luis Aparicio, Chicago White Sox
1955: Herb Score, Cleveland Indians
1954: Bob Grim, New York Yankees
1953: Harvey Kuenn, Detroit Tigers
1952: Harry Byrd, Philadelphia A's
1951: Gil McDougald, New York Yankees
1950: Walt Dropo, Boston Red Sox
1949: Roy Sievers, St. Louis Browns

Entrance to Trout Farms
(Joseph Dzidrums)

Number 27
(Joseph Dzidrums)

Essential Links

Mike's Official Twitter Account
https://twitter.com/Trouty20

Mike's Official Facebook Account
https://www.facebook.com/MikeTrout27

Mike's Official Instagram
http://instagram.com/miketrout#/

Angels Official Web Site
http://losangeles.angels.mlb.com

Official Major League Baseball Web Site
http://www.mlb.com

Angel Stadium of Anaheim
(Joseph Dzidrums)

About the Author

Christine Dzidrums has written biographies on many inspirational figures: Matt Kemp, Yasiel Puig, Mike Trout, Clayton Kershaw, Joannie Rochette, Yuna Kim, Shawn Johnson, Nastia Liukin, The Fierce Five, Gabby Douglas, Sutton Foster, Kelly Clarkson, Idina Menzel and Missy Franklin.

Christine's fictional works include: *Cutters Don't Cry*, (Moonbeam Children's Book Award), *Fair Youth*, *Timmy and the Baseball Birthday Party*, *Timmy Adopts a Girl Dog*, *Future Presidents Club* and *Princess Dessabelle Makes a Friend*.

Build Your SkateStars™
Collection Today!

At the 2010 Vancouver Olympics, tragic circumstances thrust **Joannie Rochette** into the spotlight when her mother died two days before the ladies short program. Joannie then captured hearts everywhere by courageously skating two moving programs to win the Olympic bronze medal.

Joannie Rochette: Canadian Ice Princess profiles the popular figure skater's moving journey.

Meet figure skating's biggest star: **Yuna Kim**. The Korean trailblazer produced two legendary performances at the 2010 Vancouver Olympic Games to win the gold medal. *Yuna Kim: Ice Queen* uncovers the compelling story of how the beloved figure skater overcame poor training conditions, various injuries and numerous other obstacles to become world and Olympic champion.

 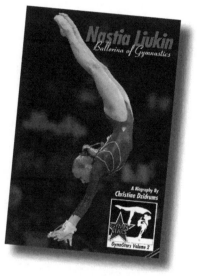

Shawn Johnson, the young woman from Des Moines, Iowa, captivated the world at the 2008 Beijing Olympics when she snagged a gold medal on the balance beam.

Shawn Johnson: Gymnastics' Golden Girl, the first volume in the **GymnStars** series, chronicles the life and career of one of sports' most beloved athletes.

Widely considered America's greatest gymnast ever, **Nastia Liukin** has inspired an entire generation with her brilliant technique, remarkable sportsmanship and unparalleled artistry.

A children's biography, *Nastia Liukin: Ballerina of Gymnastics* traces the Olympic all-around champion's ascent from gifted child prodigy to queen of her sport.

Also From

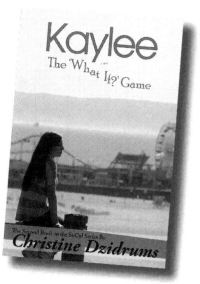

2010 Moonbeam Children's Book Award Winner! In a series of raw journal entries written to her absentee father, a teenager chronicles her penchant for self-harm, a serious struggle with depression and an inability to vocally express her feelings.

"I play the 'What If?'" game all the time. It's a cruel, wicked game."

When free spirit Kaylee suffers a devastating loss, her personality turns dark as she struggles with depression and unresolved anger. Can Kaylee repair her broken spirit, or will she remain a changed person?

Meet **Princess Dessabelle**, a spoiled, lonely princess with a quick temper. When she orders a kind classmate to be her friend, she learns the true meaning of friendship.

Build Your Timmy™
Collection Today!

Meet Timmy Martin, the world's biggest baseball fan.

One day the young boy gets invited to his cousin's birthday party. Only it's not just any old birthday party... It's a baseball birthday party!

Timmy and the Baseball Birthday Party is the first book in a series of stories featuring the world's most curious little boy!

Timmy Martin has always wanted a dog. Imagine his excitement when his mom and dad let him adopt a pet from the animal shelter. Will Timmy find the perfect dog? And will his new pet know how to play baseball?

Timmy Adopts A Girl Dog is the second story in the series about the world's most curious 4½ year old.

Twelve-year-old Emylee Markette feels invisible. Then one fateful afternoon, three beautiful sisters arrive in her sleepy New England town and instantly become the most popular girls at Forest Springs Middle School. To everyone's surprise, the Fay sisters befriend Emylee and welcome her into their close-knit circle.

Through it all, though, Emylee's weighed down by nagging suspicions. Why were the Fay sisters so anxious to befriend her? How do they know some of her inner thoughts? What do they truly want from her?

When Emylee eventually discovers that her new friends are secretly fairies, she finds her life turned upside down yet again and must make some life-changing decisions.

Fair Youth: Emylee of Forest Springs is the first book in an exciting new series for tweens!

Made in the USA
Lexington, KY
02 February 2016